LEON

Lunchbox

NATURALLY FAST RECIPES

LEON

Lunchbox

NATURALLY FAST RECIPES

By Jane Baxter, Henry Dimbleby, Kay Plunkett-Hogge,
Claire Ptak & John Vincent

PHOTOGRAPHY BY GEORGIA GLYNN SMITH · DESIGN BY ANITA MANGAN

conran
OCTOPUS

Contents

Introduction

If you ask children what was their favourite bit about their class visit to, say, the Science Museum, it isn't the space ships or the Van der Graaf generator they remember the most, it is the packed lunch.

The lunchbox has existed for generations. It is a way to refuel, yes, but really a way of expressing love. For a mum or dad it's a way of packing a parcel of pleasure to be opened half-way through the day. Farmers, labourers, postmen, tinkers and tailors have been fed by them for generations. The dude from the Deacon Blue song packs his lunch in a Sunblest bag, the New York welder ate his on a toe-tinglingly high girder and Postman Pat and Bob the Builder have both been ambassadors for the lunchbox.

There is an irony with us writing this book. For the last few years, we have been working to help children eat better in school and have created the School Food Plan – school lunches are, in almost all cases, more nutritious than packed lunches. A sandwich, a packet of crisps, a sugary yoghurt and a chocolate bar is what most parents have the time to bestow. Oh, and an apple that remains uneaten, gets brought back home every day, re-packed and then thrown away at the end of the week. Making a nutritious packed lunch is difficult – but we hope that this book will make it a little easier and give you some inspiration for those car picnics, camping trips, the working week and the odd visit to the Science Museum.

Many of the recipes in this book are suited for being prepared the night before, packed into a box or flask and eaten at work the next day. How about our tasty Ribollita on page 32? Or do you fancy a Quick Guay Tiew Nam Moo? Undecided? Then turn to page 28. You'll discover a pork meatball noodle soup that is super-quick to make, but which you will love long-time. Marion's Scotch Eggs (see page 57) will inspire you never to buy a supermarket scotch egg again. And soon you will be crowned the King, or Queen, of Slaw (see page 19). Be a good one.

Happy cooking.

Henry & John

SALADS

Salvatore's Panzanella

Panzanella is traditionally a Tuscan summer salad; however, this version comes from Salvatore, a Sicilian chef cooking in Umbria. The 'King of Pork (and cork)', as he was known to his customers, Salvatore still has a vegetable garden where he grows a huge array of some 54 types of tomato in one year. The bread used in the original version of his Panzanella was a very dry barley roll, but a dense wholemeal or sourdough loaf makes a good substitute.

250g stale **sourdough/ wholemeal bread**, ripped into 2–3cm pieces
60ml good **red wine vinegar**
60ml **olive oil**
1 clove of **garlic**, crushed
500g **cherry** or **good-quality ripe tomatoes**

salt and **freshly ground black pepper**
a bunch of **fresh basil**
1 **celery heart**, thinly sliced
1 small **red onion**, thinly sliced
50g **stoned olives**
a pinch of **dried oregano**
lots of good **olive oil**

1. Put the bread into a wide, shallow serving dish. Put the vinegar, oil and garlic into a bowl and mix together, then drizzle over the bread, mixing it in well with your hands.

2. Halve the tomatoes, sprinkle with salt and add to the bread.

3. Set aside a few leaves of basil for the garnish and scatter the rest over the bread, along with the celery, onion and olives. Sprinkle with a little pepper and oregano and drizzle with lots of good olive oil.

4. Cover the dish and set to one side in a cool place until ready to eat.

TIPS

* This is a great salad, as it can be made in advance and seems to improve with keeping.

* Panzanella can also be made with capers and roasted peppers.

Aubergines, Pomegranate & Mint

WITH A TAHINI DRESSING

SERVES 4 • PREPARATION TIME: 10 MINUTES • COOKING TIME: 10 MINUTES • ♥ ✓ WF GF DF V

Pomegranate seeds add a little sharp 'pop' to savoury dishes and are visually stunning. This dressing is also good with falafel and other vegetable fritters.

1 large **aubergine**
3 tablespoons **olive oil**
1 tablespoon good **red wine vinegar**
seeds from 1 **pomegranate**
1 tablespoon shredded **fresh mint leaves**

For the tahini dressing:
2 cloves of **garlic**, crushed
1 tablespoon **tahini**
125g **natural yoghurt**
juice of 1 **lemon**
1 tablespoon **honey**
a pinch of **cayenne pepper**
a pinch of **ground cumin**
salt and **freshly ground black pepper**

1. To make the dressing, place all the ingredients in a liquidizer (or put into a bowl and use an immersion blender) and blend together, adding a little water until you have a mixture with the consistency of double cream. Season well.

2. Slice the aubergine into discs about 5mm thick.

3. Heat the oil in a shallow frying pan, then add the aubergine slices and cook over a medium heat until lightly browned on both sides. You will need to do this in batches. When each batch is ready, remove from the pan and drain on kitchen paper.

4. Arrange the aubergine slices on a large plate. Sprinkle them with the vinegar and season well. Drizzle with the tahini dressing and scatter over the pomegranate seeds and mint.

TIPS

* To remove the seeds from a pomegranate, cut it in half across the middle. Take one half and place it cut side down on the palm of your hand. With the other hand, bash the pomegranate half with a rolling pin, quite firmly – the seeds should just come away.

French Beans & Tomatoes

WITH NIÇOISE DRESSING

SERVES 4 • PREPARATION TIME: 15 MINUTES • COOKING TIME: 3 MINUTES • ♥ ✓ WF GF DF V

If you have a few extra minutes in the morning, you could use grilled courgettes or grilled aubergines in place of the French beans in this salad.

300g **French beans**
200g **very ripe tomatoes**
1 tablespoon **capers**, soaked in lots of water
1 clove of **garlic**, crushed
1 tablespoon **red wine vinegar**
2 tablespoons **olive oil**

a small bunch of **fresh basil**
1 tablespoon **mixed olives**, chopped
3 **tomatoes**, chopped
salt and **freshly ground black pepper**

1. Top and tail the beans. Slice the tomatoes in half and extract all the juice by forcing them through a sieve into a bowl. Add the capers, garlic, vinegar, oil and basil leaves. Blend with an immersion blender or in a blender.

2. Bring a pan of salted water to the boil, then add the beans and cook for about 3 minutes, until tender (just past the squeaky stage). Drain well.

3. While the beans are still hot, toss them in a bowl with the tomato dressing, chopped olives and tomatoes. Season well.

TIPS

* If you can find them, use salted capers as they have a better flavour, but they will need soaking and rinsing before using.

* Toast some chunks of stale ciabatta in a medium-hot oven to make croûtons and toss in the tomato dressing above. Yum.

Bean, Fennel & Feta Salad

SERVES 4 • PREPARATION TIME: 10 MINUTES • COOKING TIME: 5 MINUTES • ♥ ✓ WF GF V

A simple salad.

200g **French beans**, topped
and tailed
1 head of **fennel**, trimmed
1 small bunch of **fresh flat-leaf
parsley**, leaves removed
and shredded
70g **feta cheese**, crumbled
2 tablespoons **toasted pine nuts**

For the dressing:
1 generous teaspoon **Dijon
mustard**
50ml **lemon juice**
100ml **olive oil**
salt and **freshly ground black
pepper**

1. Bring a large pan of salted water to the boil. Add the beans and
   blanch for 3–4 minutes, until tender (just past the squeaky stage).
   Set aside to cool.

2. Finely shred the fennel,
   either on a mandolin or
   using a sharp knife.

3. Whisk the dressing
   ingredients together.

4. Put the beans, fennel,
   parsley, feta and pine
   nuts into a bowl and
   mix together. Toss with
   the dressing and
   season well.

Fennel, Radish & Broad Bean Salad

SERVES 4 • PREPARATION TIME: 10 MINUTES • COOKING TIME: 5 MINUTES • ♥ WF GF DF V

An easy, pretty salad with a cooked dressing.

200g podded **broad beans**
1 tablespoon **olive oil**
salt and **freshly ground black pepper**
1 head of **fennel**
100g **radishes**
1 bunch of **watercress**

For the dressing:
60g **sesame seeds**
grated zest and juice of 1 **orange**
1 clove of **garlic**, crushed
1 tablespoon **sesame oil**
1 tablespoon **balsamic vinegar**
2 teaspoons **honey**

1. Bring a pan of salted water to the boil, then add the broad beans and cook for 2 minutes, or until tender. Drain, then put into a bowl and toss in the olive oil while still hot. Season well with salt and pepper and set aside to cool.

2. Trim the fennel and cut in half lengthways. Slice across each half very thinly. Wash the radishes and slice very thinly. Add the radishes and fennel to the bowl of broad beans.

3. Dry-fry the sesame seeds in a small non-stick frying pan over a medium heat for a few minutes, until they start to brown and pop. Quickly add the orange zest and juice and the garlic and simmer until the volume has reduced by half. Remove from the heat and add the rest of the dressing ingredients. Allow to cool, then season well.

4. Add the dressing to the bowl of vegetables and toss well. Finally, gently fold in the watercress.

TIPS

* Change the salad into a type of Middle Eastern fattoush by adding a little ground cumin to the dressing and tossing through some toasted pieces of pitta bread.

* If the broad beans are large and tough it may be necessary to peel off their outer skins.

* Grilling the fennel slightly will add a smoky flavour.

Coleslaw

SERVES 6 • PREPARATION TIME: 15 MINUTES • COOKING TIME: NONE • ✓ WF GF V

There are so many different versions of the humble coleslaw that a whole chapter could be dedicated to them. At Leon we have been playing with different mixes since the day we first opened. Here, we have given a simple recipe for a very basic slaw and followed it with three variations. If you want to experiment with your own, keep an eye on acidity (we like it sharp), seasoning, different textures and colour. Basically, however, the rules are as follows: if it tastes good raw and you can shred it, chuck it in.

½ a **white cabbage**,
　　finely shredded
300g **carrots**, peeled and grated
½ a **red onion**, very finely sliced
1 clove of **garlic**, crushed
1 tablespoon **crème fraîche**

1 tablespoon **thick natural
　　yoghurt**
1 teaspoon **Dijon mustard**
salt and **freshly ground black
　　pepper**

1. Put all the ingredients into a large bowl and mix together.
　 Season well.

COLESLAW PHOTO KEY

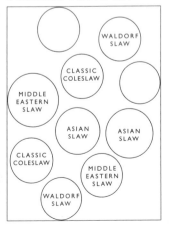

WALDORF SLAW

CLASSIC COLESLAW

MIDDLE EASTERN SLAW

ASIAN SLAW

ASIAN SLAW

CLASSIC COLESLAW

MIDDLE EASTERN SLAW

WALDORF SLAW

VARIATIONS:

Middle Eastern slaw: grated red cabbage, carrot, celeriac and squash. Dress with balsamic vinegar, olive oil and orange juice (and grated zest). Stir in toasted pine nuts, pomegranate seeds and shredded mint, and season well.

Waldorf slaw: shredded white cabbage and fennel with chopped celery and apple. Dress with pure mayonnaise or add yoghurt and crème fraîche. Fold in thinly sliced onions, toasted walnuts, golden raisins, chives and dill, and season well.

Asian slaw: shredded cabbage, thinly sliced red pepper, grated carrot, finely chopped French beans and diced tomato. Dress with lime juice, palm sugar, chopped red chilli, crushed garlic, fresh coriander and crushed peanuts.

Soba Noodle Vegetable Salad

SERVES 4 • PREPARATION TIME: 10 MINUTES • COOKING TIME: 15 MINUTES • ♥ WF DF V

Here's something you can do with peanut butter other than spreading it on toast. The vegetables used can vary with the seasons. We used broccoli and cabbage.

1 x 250g packet of **wheat-free soba noodles**
300g **broccoli florets**
½ a **Savoy cabbage**, cored and shredded

For the dressing:
120g smooth **peanut butter**
1 tablespoon **soy sauce**
2 tablespoons **warm water**
2 tablespoons **grated fresh ginger**
1 clove of **garlic**, crushed
2 tablespoons **sesame oil**
2 tablespoons **rice vinegar**
2 teaspoons **honey**
salt and **freshly ground black pepper**

1. Blend all the dressing ingredients together in a food processor or in a bowl using an immersion blender. Season.

2. Bring a large pan of salted water to the boil. Add the soba noodles and cook for about 9 minutes, until almost ready, then tip in the vegetables and cook for another 2 minutes. Drain, then transfer to a serving bowl and toss with the dressing while still hot. Serve or store for later and eat cold.

TIPS

* Try this with a mixture of the following: cauliflower, French and runner beans, sugar snap peas or grated root veg.

* This dressing also makes a good dip for grilled vegetable brochettes and kebabs.

Couscous with Seven Vegetables

SERVES 4 • PREPARATION TIME: 15 MINUTES • COOKING TIME: 40 MINUTES • ♥ DF V

In Morocco, couscous is traditionally often served with seven types of vegetables. Any variation on the seven will suffice, but it is important to add the vegetables in stages, as they will take different times to cook – that way the result won't be mush.

1 tablespoon **olive oil**
1 **onion**, diced
1 teaspoon **ground ginger**
1 teaspoon **ground cinnamon**
2 teaspoons **rose harissa**
1 x 400g tin of **chopped tomatoes**
1kg **mixed vegetables** (six types – we used **squash**, **turnips**, **parsnips**, **carrots**, all peeled and cut into small chunks; **courgettes**, halved and sliced; **French beans**, trimmed)
100ml **water**
salt and **freshly ground black pepper**
1 x 400g tin of **chickpeas**, drained
juice of 1 **orange**
chopped **fresh coriander and mint**

For the couscous:
200g **couscous**
1 tablespoon **olive oil**
400ml **boiling water**

1. Heat the oil in a large pan, then add the onion and cook over a medium heat for 5 minutes.

2. Add the spices and harissa and stir well. Cook for 1 minute, then add the tomatoes with their juice. Bring up to a simmer and tip in the squash and the root vegetables. Add the 100ml water, stir and season well. Bring up to a simmer, then cover and cook over a low heat for 15 minutes, or until the vegetables are almost tender.

3. Add the rest of the vegetables and cook for a further 10 minutes, pouring in a little more water if the mixture starts to stick.

4. When all the vegetables are tender, add the drained chickpeas, the orange juice, then season and mix well.

5. To cook the couscous, put the grain into a bowl and rub in the olive oil and a little salt. Pour over the boiling water, then cover tightly with clingfilm and leave to steam for 10 minutes.

6. Fluff up the couscous with a fork, sprinkle with the chopped herbs, then serve with the vegetables.

TIPS

* Traditionally dried fruit and nuts are added to meat tagines, so try adding sliced dried apricots or dates for an authentic flavour. Toasted almonds, pine nuts or cashews are also nice additions.

* The types of vegetables used can be varied, but it is good to try and maintain a balance of root and green veg. Other vegetables you could use include: cauliflower, broccoli, spinach, kale, celeriac or mushrooms.

'Rubies in the Sand' Salad

SERVES 4 • PREPARATION TIME: 25 MINUTES • COOKING TIME: 20–25 MINUTES • ♥ ✓ WF GF DF V

Quinoa is one of our great favourites. It contains no gluten and is a complete protein – ideal for vegetarians.

200g **dried quinoa**
300g **mixed peppers** (yellow, orange, red), deseeded and halved
2–3 sprigs of **fresh thyme**
2 cloves of **garlic**, unpeeled, crushed
1 tablespoon **olive oil**
a good handful of **fresh coriander**, chopped
100g **pomegranate seeds**

For the dressing:
2 tablespoons **extra virgin olive oil**
the juice of 1 **lime** or ½ **lemon**
2 teaspoons **ras al hanout**
salt and **freshly ground black pepper**

1. Wash the quinoa thoroughly, then cook it as per the instructions on the packet. Some bought quinoa is pre-soaked, some not, so you need to check. Once the quinoa is cooked, drain and set aside to cool.

2. Meanwhile, heat the oven to 180°C/350°F/gas mark 4.

3. Pop the peppers on to a roasting tray with the thyme, garlic and olive oil. Roast in the oven for about 20–25 minutes, or until al dente. Remove from the oven, discard the garlic and thyme, then set aside to cool. Chop the peppers into 2cm squares.

4. Mix the cooled quinoa with the mixed peppers, the chopped coriander and the pomegranate seeds.

5. Mix all the dressing ingredients together thoroughly. Stir into the quinoa mix. Taste and season with salt and pepper if needed.

TIPS

* Ras al hanout is a mixed spice quite readily available in most supermarkets. It's Moroccan in origin and contains cardamom, cloves, chilli, cumin and cinnamon, among other spices.

* Try this with about 100g of gently fried crispy chorizo scattered on top.

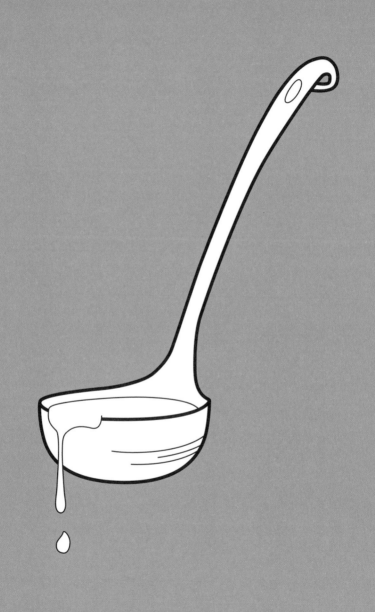

SOUPS
& STEWS

Quick Guay Tiew Nam Moo

(PORK MEATBALL NOODLE SOUP)

A super-quick shortcut to a tasty Thai pork noodle soup. You can find variations on this theme on practically every street corner in Thailand. To be honest, it's perfect at any time of day, not just lunch. And it's great for the morning after the night before …

For the meatballs:
1 teaspoon **white peppercorns**
2 fresh **coriander roots**
2 cloves of **garlic**
a pinch of **salt**
200g **minced pork**
a dash of **nam pla** (fish sauce)

For the soup:
100g medium-width **rice noodles**
1 tablespoon **vegetable oil**
1 clove of **garlic**, smashed
1.2 litres **stock**, any flavour
2 tablespoons **light soy sauce**
2 tablespoons **nam pla** (fish sauce)
100g **bean sprouts**
100g **pak choi** (about 1 head), roughly chopped
3 **spring onions**, trimmed and finely chopped
a handful of **fresh coriander leaves**, chopped

1. Fill a large bowl with water and pop in your rice noodles; this just softens them and gets rid of a lot of the starch, which would otherwise make your soup 'gummy'.

2. In a pestle and mortar, pound the peppercorns, coriander roots, garlic and the salt to a paste. Then, in a clean bowl, mix the paste with the minced pork and nam pla, mushing it thoroughly with your hands. Form the mixture into 16 meatballs and set them aside.

3. Now for the soup. Heat the oil in a large saucepan and, once it's hot, add the smashed clove of garlic. Cook for a minute or so until it's really fragrant – but don't let it colour. Pour in the stock and bring to the boil. Add the soy sauce and the nam pla, bring it back to the boil, then add the meatballs. When they're cooked through – in about a minute or two – add your drained noodles.

4. Bring it all back to the boil and add your bean sprouts and pak choi. Bring back to the boil again and cook for 3 minutes. Check that the noodles are cooked – by this time your vegetables will be ready. You want them with a little bite.

5. Divide between bowls and top each bowl with a few spring onion bits and some chopped coriander.

TIPS

* In Thailand, you get this served with a selection of condiments called *kruang prung*. These could be some ground, roasted dried chillies, rice vinegar with mild chillies sliced into it, nam pla with finely sliced bird's-eye chillies; lime juice; sugar; plain nam pla and crushed peanuts.

Rasam

SERVES 6 · PREPARATION TIME: 10 MINUTES · COOKING TIME: 40 MINUTES · ♥ ✓ WF GF DF V

Rasam is a South Indian soup that can be eaten either with rice or on its own.

50g **red lentils**
1 teaspoon **black peppercorns**
2 teaspoons **cumin seeds**
3 **dried red chillies**
2 cloves of **garlic**, crushed
750g ripe **tomatoes**, chopped
1 tablespoon **sunflower oil**

1 teaspoon **mustard seeds**
10 **curry leaves**
a pinch of **ground turmeric**
2 teaspoons **tamarind paste**
750ml **water**
salt and **freshly ground black pepper**

1. Wash the lentils and put them into a pan. Cover them with water and cook over a medium heat for 20 minutes, or until soft. Remove from the heat and set aside.

2. Dry-roast the peppercorns, cumin seeds and chillies in a small frying pan over a medium heat for 2 minutes. Grind them together in a pestle and mortar or let them cool a little and grind in a spice grinder to a powder. Mix them with the crushed garlic to form a paste, then set aside.

3. Blend the tomatoes in a liquidizer or food processor.

4. Heat the oil in a large pan and add the mustard seeds and curry leaves. Cook over a medium heat until the seeds start to pop, then add the tomatoes and turmeric.

5. Add the lentils, spice paste, tamarind and water and bring to a simmer. Cook over a low heat for 15 minutes, then pass through a sieve or food mill. Season well.

Corn Chowder

SERVES 4 • PREPARATION TIME: 15 MINUTES • COOKING TIME: 40 MINUTES • WF GF V

Another soup for an autumn day, when corn is plentiful.

50g **butter**
2 **onions**, finely chopped
2 cloves of **garlic**, crushed
2 **red chillies**, chopped
a sprig of **fresh thyme** (or a
   pinch of dried thyme)
a good pinch of **ground cumin**
a good pinch of **smoked paprika**
1 **red pepper**, finely chopped
4 cobs of **sweetcorn**

2 **baking potatoes** (about 400g),
   peeled and cut into 1cm dice
a splash of **white wine**
   (about 50ml)
500ml **milk** (soya milk can
   be used)
250ml **water**
salt and **freshly ground black
   pepper**

1. Melt the butter in a large pan over a low heat. Add the onions, garlic, chillies, thyme, spices and red pepper and cook for 10 minutes, stirring occasionally.

2. Remove the kernels from the sweetcorn cobs by standing them upright on a chopping board and cutting downwards with a sawing action. Add the kernels to the pan and turn up the heat, stirring constantly for 5 minutes so that the corn browns slightly, but be careful not to let it burn.

3. Add the diced potatoes, followed by the wine, and turn up the heat. Cook rapidly for 1 minute.

4. Pour in the milk and bring to a simmer. Cook over a low heat for 10 minutes, then add the water, bring the chowder back to a simmer and continue to cook for a further 10 minutes, or until the potatoes are tender and the soup begins to thicken. Season well.

Ribollita

This is a hearty Tuscan soup that literally means 'reboiled'. It is a creative way of using up stale bread, something the Italians do so well. If you have time to cook the vegetables for longer at the start, the soup will be better for it.

2 tablespoons **olive oil**
1 **onion**, finely chopped
3 sticks of **celery**, finely chopped
1 large **carrot**, chopped
a pinch of **dried chilli**
a pinch of **wild oregano** (optional)
3 cloves of **garlic**, crushed
¼ of a **Savoy cabbage** (or other cabbage), cored and shredded
1 x 400g tin of **chopped tomatoes**

salt and **freshly ground black pepper**
1 x 400g tin of **borlotti beans** (or white beans), drained
300g **black kale**, de-stemmed and shredded
400ml **boiling water**
200g stale **ciabatta**, broken into 2–3cm chunks
extra virgin olive oil, to serve

1. Heat the olive oil in a large pan and add the onion, celery and carrot. Cook for 10 minutes over a low heat, then add the chilli, oregano and garlic and cook for 2 more minutes, stirring well.

2. Add the shredded cabbage and tomatoes, season, stir well and cook over a high heat for 5 minutes.

3. Add the beans and shredded kale and pour in the boiling water. Stir, then bring to a simmer and cook for another 5 minutes, or until the kale is tender.

4. Remove a cupful of the soup and blend well in a liquidizer or food processor, then stir it back into the soup in the pan.

5. Bring the soup back to a simmer, then remove from the heat and fold in the chunks of bread. Drizzle with lots of extra virgin olive oil and check the seasoning.

TIPS

* The base for this soup makes a good minestrone, so you could add cooked small pasta or macaroni instead of the bread.

Courgette Soup

This soup is equally good hot or cold, depending on the season.

550g **courgettes**
1 large **onion**
30g **butter**
750ml **chicken stock**
sea salt and **freshly ground black pepper**

1. Trim and slice the courgettes. Finely chop the onion.

2. Melt the butter in a large saucepan. Add the onion and sauté gently for about 5 minutes, or until soft but not brown.

3. Add the courgettes, stir for a minute, then add the stock and bring to the boil. Cover and simmer gently for 30 minutes.

4. Whizz with a hand blender or in a food processor and season with salt and pepper to taste. Eat hot, or cold from the fridge in summer.

Chilled Cucumber Soup

SERVES 4 • PREPARATION TIME: 10 MINUTES, PLUS CHILLING • COOKING TIME: NONE • ♥ ✓ WF GF V

A lovely, quick, cooling soup for a hot summer's day ... let's hope we have some of those.

1kg **cucumbers**, peeled and deseeded
½ a **red onion**, finely chopped
2 cloves of **garlic**, crushed
1 **green chilli**, deseeded and chopped
2 tablespoons chopped **fresh mint leaves**
juice of 1 **lemon**
2 teaspoons **honey**
50ml **olive oil**
150g **natural yoghurt**
100–150ml **water**
salt

1. Put all the ingredients into a food processor and blend until the soup is very smooth. If necessary, add more water to thin the soup down to your desired consistency.

2. Transfer to a bowl and chill for at least 2 hours.

Gazpacho

SERVES 2 • PREPARATION TIME: 10 MINUTES, PLUS CHILLING • COOKING TIME: NONE
♥ ✓ WF GF DF V

This recipe does not involve deseeding and peeling the tomatoes, but for a smoother result, pass the gazpacho through a mouli-légumes (or a food mill).

1–2 **green peppers**, deseeded
8 juicy red **tomatoes**
1 **cucumber**, peeled
4 cloves of **garlic**, crushed
4 tablespoons very good **olive oil**
2 tablespoons **white wine vinegar**
salt

1. Put all the ingredients into a liquidizer and blend until smooth.

2. Check the seasoning, and add more olive oil or white wine vinegar according to taste.

3. Transfer to a bowl and chill for at least 2 hours, longer if possible – this soup will definitely improve with keeping and would travel well in a thermos flask.

TIPS

*   If you want to serve it quickly, add a few ice cubes to the mix before you blend it.

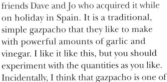

This recipe was given to me by my friends Dave and Jo who acquired it while on holiday in Spain. It is a traditional, simple gazpacho that they like to make with powerful amounts of garlic and vinegar. I like it like this, but you should experiment with the quantities as you like. Incidentally, I think that gazpacho is one of the few worthwhile uses for a green pepper.

HENRY

Squash, Corn & Bean Stew

SERVES 4 • PREPARATION TIME: 15 MINUTES • COOKING TIME: 30 MINUTES • ♥ WF GF DF V

The stuff of bonfires and chilly days. This can be let down with a little vegetable stock and turned into a soup. It's great with tortilla chips sprinkled on top.

2 tablespoons **olive oil**
2 medium **onions**, chopped
1 **red pepper**, chopped
3 cloves of **garlic**, crushed
1 teaspoon **ground cumin**
2 teaspoons **ground paprika**
2 cobs of **sweetcorn**, kernels removed
400g **butternut squash**, peeled and cut into small dice
4 large **tomatoes**, roughly chopped
salt and **freshly ground black pepper**
250ml **vegetable stock**
1 x 440g tin of **pinto beans** (or **borlotti** or **cannellini beans**), drained

1. Heat the oil in a large saucepan over a medium heat. Add the onions, red pepper and garlic and cook for 5 minutes.

2. Add the spices, corn kernels, squash and tomatoes and mix well. Cook for another 5 minutes, stirring to make sure the vegetables doesn't stick to the pan. Season well.

3. Add the stock and bring to a simmer, then cover the pan and cook gently over a low heat for 20 minutes, or until the squash is tender. (Add more stock or water if required.)

4. Stir in the drained beans and warm through. Season well.

TIPS

* We have used butternut squash which is easy to prepare, but other squashes and pumpkins work well.

* Try adding a chopped fresh red chilli in step 1 if you like it hot.

TARTS & FRITTATAS

French Onion Tart

SERVES 4 • PREPARATION TIME: 30 MINUTES, PLUS RESTING • COOKING TIME: 25–30 MINUTES • ♥

This recipe is an adaptation of the French classic pissaladiere, but made with spelt flour. It is very simple and very versatile. The possibilities for alternative toppings are endless.

For the spelt pastry:
125g **plain spelt flour**
a pinch of **salt**
a pinch of **sugar**
100g cold **unsalted butter**, cut into pieces
4 tablespoons **iced water**

For the topping:
3 tablespoons **olive oil**
2 **onions**, thinly sliced
1 teaspoon **vinegar**
2 teaspoons of **water**
a small bunch of **fresh thyme**
50g **black** or **niçoise olives**
6 **anchovies**
salt and **freshly ground black pepper**
1 **free-range egg**, beaten

1. To make the spelt pastry, combine the spelt flour, salt and sugar in a bowl and cut in the butter with a knife. Leave larger chunks of butter than you would think (about the size of a garlic clove) to make the pastry more flaky.

2. Drizzle in the water and bring it all together in a ball.

3. Wrap the pastry in clingfilm, and let it rest in the fridge for at least 30 minutes.

4. Meanwhile, make the topping. Heat the oil in a heavy-based saucepan and add the sliced onions. Stir occasionally to be sure they don't burn. You are looking for a caramelized but soft onion.

5. Once cooked (about 7 or 8 minutes) add the vinegar and 2 teaspoons of water. Sprinkle with thyme leaves and transfer into a bowl to cool.

6. Heat the oven to 160°C/325°F/gas mark 3.

7. Pit and break up the olives a little. On a floured surface roll out the dough to approximately 3mm thick and transfer to a baking sheet. Arrange the cooled onions, anchovies and olives over the dough, leaving a small border, and season with salt and pepper.

8. Brush the edges with beaten egg, then bake the tart in the oven for 25–30 minutes.

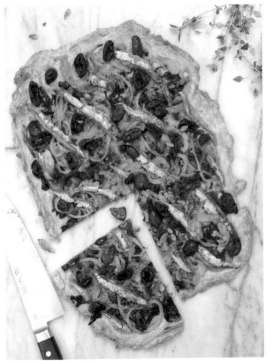

VARIATIONS:

Buffalo tart: Onions, slices of buffalo mozzarella and tomato. Basil. Drizzle of olive oil.

Sausage & sage tart: Onions and bits of sausage and chopped sage.

Tomato & thyme tart: Fine layer of Dijon mustard. Onions and slices of tomato. Thyme.

Broccoli & goat's cheese tart: Onions. Finely chopped pieces of broccoli. Crumble on goat's cheese after cooking.

Tomato, Thyme & Goat's Cheese Tart

SERVES 4–6 • PREPARATION TIME: 15 MINUTES • COOKING TIME: 20–25 MINUTES • V

You can whip this up in minutes, making it the perfect quick lunch.

1 sheet of **ready-rolled puff pastry**
2 tablespoons **extra virgin olive oil**
400g **cherry tomatoes**, halved, or **small tomatoes**, quartered
4 sprigs of **fresh thyme**, leaves picked
1 clove of **garlic**, peeled and chopped
salt and **freshly ground black pepper**
80g **soft goat's cheese**

1. Heat the oven to 220°C/425°F/gas mark 7.

2. Lay out the puff pastry on a baking tray lined with baking paper. Then, using a sharp knife, score a line – not all the way through – down and across each side of the pastry, about 2cm in from the edges. This will give the tart a nice crusty raised edge.

3. Put the olive oil, cherry tomatoes, thyme leaves and garlic into a bowl and mix until they are well coated. Season with salt and pepper and mix again.

4. Tumble the tomato mixture evenly over the pastry, keeping it within the lines.

5. Crumble the goat's cheese over the top among the bits of tomato.

6. Add another quick dash of freshly ground pepper and pop it into the oven for about 20 minutes, or until it's golden brown and puffy on the outside and the tomatoes are collapsing slightly and the cheese is melt-y.

TIPS

* For something a little sweeter, you could replace the tomatoes with sliced fresh figs. Keep everything else the same – just add a good drizzle of runny honey before serving.

Chard & Bacon Tart

SERVES 6–8 • PREPARATION TIME: 25 MINUTES • COOKING TIME: 40–50 MINUTES

The marriage of cream, bacon, chard and cheese sits happily-ever-after in a crisp pastry shell. One of our more indulgent favourites. What's more, you don't need to roll out the pastry either …

70g **lardons** or chopped **bacon**
1 tablespoon **olive oil**
1 clove of **garlic**, peeled and finely sliced
100g **chard leaves** or **kale**, shredded
salt and **freshly ground black pepper**
2 **free-range eggs**, lightly beaten
1 **egg yolk**
200ml **double cream**

100g **Gruyère cheese**
1–2 sprigs of **fresh thyme**, leaves picked

For the pastry:
250g **plain flour**
125g **unsalted butter**, straight from the fridge, diced
a good pinch of **sea salt**
a small glass of **iced water**

1. Heat the oven to 200°C/400°F/gas mark 6. Butter a 23cm round, non-stick tart tin with a removable base.

2. First make your pastry. Measure out the flour into a large bowl and add the butter. Start rubbing the flour and butter together with your fingertips, lifting it and gently working it until you have what looks like fine breadcrumbs.

3. Add the salt. Then add the iced water a teaspoonful at a time, until the pastry just comes together. Don't add too much water or you'll get a hard pastry.

4. Roll it into a loose ball and, using your fingertips, gently push the dough into the prepared tart tin, easing it around until it evenly covers the base and sides. Cover the whole thing with a sheet of greaseproof paper and weight it down with some baking beans. Then bake it in the oven for 10 minutes.

5. Over a medium heat, cook the lardons or chopped bacon in a frying pan until cooked through, about 5 minutes. Remove with a slotted spoon and set aside.

6. Wipe out the pan, then return it to the heat and add the olive oil. Add the garlic. Fry for a minute or so – don't let it colour too much – then add the chard and a pinch of salt, and cook until it is just wilted. Remove from the heat, set aside and leave to drain in a colander. Then, when it's cool, squeeze out any excess liquid.

7. Take the tart shell out of the oven. Carefully remove the greaseproof paper and the baking beans, and pop it back into the oven for another 5 minutes to crisp up.

8. In a clean bowl, beat the eggs, egg yolk, cream, salt and pepper with an electric whisk. Stir in the Gruyère and the thyme leaves and season with salt and pepper.

9. Remove the tart shell from the oven. Scatter the chard across the base. Sprinkle the bacon bits in, then pour in the cream and egg mixture.

10. Bake the tart in the oven for about 30–40 minutes, until the filling has puffed up and the pastry is a lovely golden brown.

Hattie's Sweet Onion Frittata

SERVES 4 • PREPARATION TIME: 15 MINUTES • COOKING TIME: 30 MINUTES • ♥ WF GF V

This is a very economical and cheap lunch to have with salad and a chunk of bread.

800g **onions**
a handful of **fresh flat-leaf parsley**
50g **butter**
8 **large free-range eggs**
sea salt and **freshly ground black pepper**

1. Peel the onions and slice into thin semi-circles. Roughly chop the parsley. Melt the butter in a large frying pan and add the onions. Cook over a gentle heat, covered with a lid if you have one, for 25 minutes, or until the onions are soft and sweet. Meanwhile, heat the grill to a medium heat.

2. Crack the eggs into a bowl and mix well, adding salt and pepper to taste.

3. Add the onion mixture to the eggs, mix well and add the chopped parsley. Return the mixture to the pan that the onions were cooking in, or a smaller one if the original is wide and will make the frittata too shallow.

4. Very gently cook the frittata on the hob, watching carefully so as not to let it burn on the bottom. When you think it's cooked through, apart from the top, which will still be runny, place it under the grill to finish off the top.

5. Allow to cool to lukewarm, and have with a green salad.

TIPS

* Grated Parmesan is a good addition to the egg mixture. You can mix any leftover vegetables with the onions, too. Peas and peppers go well, as do cold potatoes and any old ends of cheese that you might want to use up.

* To make this into a quiche or tart, line a 25cm flan tin with puff or shortcrust pastry (if using short crust pastry you will need to bake it blind for 15 minutes in the preheated oven first). Add the onion filling and bake it in the oven at 180°C/350°F/gas mark 4 for 25–30 minutes, or until golden and firm.

Asparagus & Wild Garlic Frittata

SERVES 4 • PREPARATION TIME: 10 MINUTES • COOKING TIME: 10 MINUTES • WF GF V

Asparagus and wild garlic have roughly the same season, and this is a simple lunch using both. Fresh mint or basil can be used instead of the garlic leaves.

350–400g **asparagus**
6 **free-range eggs**
1 tablespoon **white wine**
2 tablespoons grated vegetarian **pecorino or Parmesan-style cheese**

salt and **freshly ground black pepper**
1 tablespoon **olive oil**
1 clove of **garlic**, crushed
a small bunch of **fresh wild garlic leaves**, washed and shredded

1. To prepare the asparagus, first snap off and discard the woody ends. Cut the asparagus into 2–3cm lengths. Bring a large pan of salted water to the boil, add the asparagus, blanch for 2 minutes and drain.

2. Put the eggs into a bowl with the white wine and 1 tablespoon of grated pecorino and whisk together. Season well.

3. Heat the grill. Heat the olive oil in a 22–24cm non-stick frying pan. Add the asparagus, garlic and wild garlic leaves and sauté over a medium heat for 2 minutes, then lower the heat.

4. Pour in the egg mixture and draw in from the sides with a wooden spoon to allow the uncooked egg to run underneath.

5. Cook gently for 5 minutes. Sprinkle with the rest of the cheese and flash under the hot grill to finish cooking the top.

6. Slide from the pan on to a large plate and cut into wedges.

VARIATIONS:
Broccoli frittata: Purple sprouting broccoli can be substituted for the asparagus.
Aubergine frittata: Try using diced aubergine or courgettes, but do not cook them in boiling water – instead sauté them lightly in olive oil before adding to the egg mix.
Onion and pepper frittata: Sautéd onions and red peppers make a delicious frittata, so cook them with a little vinegar and sugar and add lots of shredded basil to the egg mix.

SANDWICHES & SMALL BITES

Ploughman's in a Box

That great British pub staple – a perfect portable feast.

> 250g **Cheddar cheese**
> 4 fat slices of good **ham**
> 2 large **pickled onions**
> 2 **crisp apples** (we love Cox's)
> 2 slices of your favourite **bread**
> 50g **unsalted butter**
> 2 sticks of **celery**, trimmed
> a splodge of **Branston pickle**, or homemade **chutney** of your choice
> **salt** and **freshly ground black pepper**
> a pint of **shandy** (optional)

1. Find a lovely box – something vintage would be great, but Tupperware or brown cardboard is just as good. Arrange everything, except the shandy, snugly inside. Tie up with string.

2. Chill the shandy.

3. Picnic.

TIPS

* Feel free to replace the Cheddar with your favourite cheese: we are fans of Stilton or Wensleydale.

* Add some spring onions if you like, and some wedges of crisp lettuce or endive.

Diamond Jubilee Chicken Sarnie

SERVES 4 • PREPARATION TIME: 15 MINUTES • COOKING TIME: NONE • ♥

This updated Leon version is based on a classic: Rosemary Hume and Constance Spry's world-famous Coronation Chicken, created in 1953 for the Coronation of Queen Elizabeth II. As an homage to the wonderful multicultural Caribbean, we've tweaked it to make a lighter, spikier sandwich.

2 tablespoons **thick yoghurt**
1 tablespoon good **mayonnaise**
2 teaspoons **curry powder**
salt and **freshly ground black pepper**
300g cold **roast chicken**
4 slices from your favourite **bread**

For the mango salsa:
2 ripe **mangoes**, peeled, stoned and cubed
a good squeeze of **fresh lime juice**
¼ of a **Scotch bonnet chilli**, deseeded and chopped
½ a **red onion**, finely diced
a good handful of **fresh coriander**, finely chopped
salt and **freshly ground black pepper**

1. Gently mix the yoghurt, mayonnaise, curry powder, salt and pepper together in a large bowl. Taste. Add more seasoning if needed.

2. Stir in the shredded roast chicken and coat well. Pop into a Tupperware container for travel.

3. To make the salsa, just mix all the ingredients together, taste for seasoning and place in a separate Tupperware or jar.

4. To put the Jubilee Sandwich together, first put celebratory crowns on heads.

5. Pile the curried chicken mixture on to your slices of bread.

6. Top with the mango salsa.

Marion's Scotch Eggs

SERVES 6 • PREPARATION TIME: 20 MINUTES • COOKING TIME: 15 MINUTES • ✓ DF

John's mum Marion (Leon's wife) is the mistress of Scotch eggs. They would either eat them warm (lovely), or take them to the Essex coast on weekend trips. He still doesn't know whether they are best eaten whole (in many bites, not all at once) or cut in half. The only solution is to have two – one whole, one cut in two.

6 **free-range eggs**
500g **sausage meat**
sea salt and **freshly ground black pepper**
2 teaspoons **English mustard**
2 handfuls of **fresh breadcrumbs**
4 tablespoons **vegetable oil**

1. Hard-boil the eggs, then shell them and dry with kitchen paper.

2. Season the meat with salt and pepper and add the mustard.

3. Using wet hands, divide the sausage meat into 6 egg-sized balls.

4. Spread the breadcrumbs in a dish.

5. Take a ball of sausage meat and spread it out into a disc in the palm of your hand. Lay an egg on it and gently work the sausage meat until it smoothly encases the egg. Drop it into the breadcrumbs and roll it around until covered.

6. Heat the oil in a pan and gently fry the Scotch eggs until golden brown all over.

TIPS

* If you want to show off, boil the eggs so that the yolks are still slightly soft.
* You could use duck's or quail's eggs to make alternative sized Scotch eggs.
* Some books will tell you to deep-fry them – no, no, we disagree.

Egyptian Falafels

MAKES ABOUT 16 (ENOUGH FOR 3–4) • PREPARATION TIME: 20 MINUTES, PLUS SOAKING & COOLING
COOKING TIME: 10 MINUTES • WF GF

Surprisingly easy to cook from scratch, this traditional Arab food is delicious as a lunch-time snack. Authentic Egyptian falafels are made with fava beans, not chickpeas. Unlike many others, our falafels are both gluten-free and vegan.

500g **split dried fava beans**
a big bunch of **fresh coriander**
10 **fresh mint leaves**
1 **red chilli**
1 **red onion**
1 teaspoon **cayenne pepper**
1 teaspoon **ground cumin**
½ teaspoon **ground cinnamon**
3 pinches of **coarse salt**

3 pinches of **freshly ground black pepper**
grated zest of 2 **lemons**
vegetable oil, for deep-frying

For the mint yoghurt sauce:
8 **fresh mint leaves**
350g **natural yoghurt**
juice of ½ a **lemon**

1. You need to soak the beans overnight, but don't boil them, as all the cooking happens in the oil. Drain the beans after soaking.

2. Coarsely chop the herbs, chilli and onion. Put into a food processor with the beans, spices, salt, pepper and lemon zest, then pulse until fairly smooth – though not a paste.

3. Roll the mixture into ping-pong ball sized patties, place on a plate, then refrigerate for 30 minutes.

4. Meanwhile, prepare the yoghurt sauce. Finely chop the mint and mix in a bowl with the yoghurt and lemon juice. Season with salt and pepper, then refrigerate until ready to serve.

5. Heat enough vegetable oil in a wide deep pan big enough to fit all the patties in a single layer. When the oil is very hot (about 180°C), carefully lower the patties in the oil and deep-fry for 3–4 minutes, or until dark golden brown.

6. Drain briefly on kitchen paper and sprinkle lightly with salt. Have the falafel with the yoghurt sauce, a lightly dressed salad and some pitta bread.

Spicy Chicken Drumsticks

SERVES 4 • PREPARATION TIME: 3 MINUTES • COOKING TIME: 45 MINUTES • ✓ WF GF DF

These could not be more simple. A perfect thing to store in the fridge to pick on when hunger strikes at lunch time.

8 **chicken drumsticks**
1 tablespoon **extra virgin olive oil**
1 tablespoon **runny honey**
2 teaspoons **mild curry powder**
sea salt and **freshly ground black pepper**
½ a **lemon**

1. Heat the oven to 240°C/475°F/gas mark 9.

2. Lay a sheet of foil in a baking tray, leaving a little excess sticking up around the sides.

3. With a sharp knife, slash the sides of the chicken drumsticks – this will allow the flavours to seep in and the meat to cook evenly.

4. Put the chicken in a bowl and add the oil, honey and curry powder and mix well to coat the chicken. Then tip the chicken onto the baking tray and add some salt and pepper. Pop into the oven for 45 minutes, turning the drumsticks every 15 minutes or so.

5. Take out of the oven, leave to cool for a few minutes, then douse with a squeeze of lemon.

CONVERSION CHART FOR COMMON MEASURE

LIQUIDS

15 ml	$^1/_2$ fl oz
25 ml	1 fl oz
50 ml	2 fl oz
75 ml	3 fl oz
100 ml	3 $^1/_2$ fl oz
125 ml	4 fl oz
150 ml	$^1/_4$ pint
175 ml	6 fl oz
200 ml	7 fl oz
250 ml	8 fl oz
275 ml	9 fl oz
300 ml	$^1/_2$ pint
325 ml	11 fl oz
350 ml	12 fl oz
375 ml	13 fl oz
400 ml	14 fl oz
450 ml	$^3/_4$ pint
475 ml	16 fl oz
500 ml	17 fl oz
575 ml	18 fl oz
600 ml	1 pint
750 ml	1 $^1/_4$ pints
900 ml	1 $^1/_2$ pints
1 litre	1 $^3/_4$ pints
1.2 litres	2 pints
1.5 litres	2 $^1/_2$ pints
1.8 litres	3 pints
2 litres	3 $^1/_2$ pints
2.5 litres	4 pints
3.6 litres	6 pints

WEIGHTS

5 g	$^1/_4$ oz
15 g	$^1/_2$ oz
20 g	$^3/_4$ oz
25 g	1 oz
50 g	2 oz
75 g	3 oz
125 g	4 oz
150 g	5 oz
175 g	6 oz
200 g	7 oz
250 g	8 oz
275 g	9 oz
300 g	10 oz
325 g	11 oz
375 g	12 oz
400 g	13 oz
425 g	14 oz
475 g	15 oz
500 g	1 lb
625 g	1 $^1/_4$ lb
750 g	1 $^1/_2$ lb
875 g	1 $^3/_4$ lb
1 kg	2 lb
1.25 kg	2 $^1/_2$ lb
1.5 kg	3 lb
1.75 kg	3 $^1/_2$ lb
2 kg	4 lb

OVEN TEMPERATURES

110°C......(225°F).......Gas Mark 1/4
120°C......(250°F).......Gas Mark 1/2
140°C......(275°F).......Gas Mark 1
150°C......(300°F).......Gas Mark 2
160°C......(325°F).......Gas Mark 3
180°C......(350°F).......Gas Mark 4
190°C......(375°F).......Gas Mark 5
200°C......(400°F).......Gas Mark 6
220°C......(425°F).......Gas Mark 7
230°C......(450°F).......Gas Mark 8

MEASUREMENTS

5 mm	1/4 inch
1 cm	1/2 inch
1.5 cm	3/4 inch
2.5 cm	1 inch
5 cm	2 inches
7 cm	3 inches
10 cm	4 inches
12 cm	5 inches
15 cm	6 inches
18 cm	7 inches
20 cm	8 inches
23 cm	9 inches
25 cm	10 inches
28 cm	11 inches
30 cm	12 inches
33 cm	13 inches

Working with different types of oven

All the recipes in this book have been tested in an oven without a fan. If you are using a fan-assisted oven, lower the temperature given in the recipe by 20°C. Modern fan-assisted ovens are very efficient at circulating heat evenly around the oven, so there's also no need to worry about positioning.

Regardless of what type of oven you use you will find that it has its idiosyncrasies, so don't stick slavishly to any baking recipes. Make sure you understand how your oven behaves and adjust accordingly.

KEY TO SYMBOLS / NUTRITIONAL INFO

♥   LOW SATURATED FATS

✓   LOW GLYCAEMIC (GI) LOAD

WF   WHEAT FREE

GF   GLUTEN FREE

DF   DAIRY FREE

V   VEGETARIAN

   COOKING TIPS, EXTRA INFORMATION
TIPS AND ALTERNATIVE IDEAS.

Index

An Hachette UK Company
www.hachette.co.uk

First published in Great Britain in 2015
by Conran Octopus Limited, a part of
Octopus Publishing Group, Carmelite House,
50 Victoria Embankment, London EC4Y 0DZ
www.octopusbooks.co.uk

This book includes a selection of previously
published recipes taken from the following
titles: *Leon Naturally Fast Food*, *Leon Baking
& Puddings*, *Leon Family & Friends* and *Leon
Fast Vegetarian*.

Publisher: Alison Starling
Managing Editor: Sybella Stephens
Assistant Editor: Meri Pentikäinen
Art Director: Jonathan Christie
Art Direction, Design and Illustrations:
  Anita Mangan
Design Assistant: Abigail Read
Photography: Georgia Glynn Smith
Production Controller: Allison Gonsalves

ISBN 978 1 84091 704 8

Printed and bound in China

10 9 8 7 6 5 4 3 2 1

A note from the authors …
Medium eggs should be used unless
otherwise stated.
We have endeavoured to be as accurate as
possible in all the preparation and cooking
times listed in the recipes in this book.
However, they are an estimate based on our
own timings during recipe testing, and should
be taken as a guide only, not as the literal
truth. We have also tried to source all our
food facts carefully, but we are not scientists.
So our food facts and nutrition advice are not
absolute. If you feel you require consultation
with a nutritionist, consult your GP for a
recommendation.

Also available in the Little Leon series …

Breakfast & Brunch • *Smoothies, Juices & Cocktails*
Soups, Salads & Snacks • *Brownies, Bars & Muffins*
Fast Suppers • *One Pot* • *Sweet Treats*